# 50 Things to Know About Working with Millennials

## 50 Travel Tips from a Local

Isla Bishop

Copyright © 2017 CZYK Publishing

All Rights Reserved. No part of this publication may be reproduced, including scanning and photocopying, or distributed in any form or by any means, electronic or mechanical, or stored in a database or retrieval system without prior written permission from the publisher.

Disclaimer: The publisher has put forth an effort in preparing and arranging this book. The information provided herein by the author is provided "as is". Use this information at your own risk. Consult your doctor before engaging in any medical activities. The publisher and author disclaim any liabilities for any loss of profit or commercial or personal damages resulting from the information contained in this book.

Order Information: To order this title please email lbrenenc@gmail.com or visit GreaterThanATourist.com. A bulk discount can be provided.

Cover Template Creator: Lisa Rusczyk Ed. D. using Canva.
Cover Creator:
Image:

Lock Haven, PA
All rights reserved.
**ISBN:** 9781522078494

# BOOK DESCRIPTION

Do you want to identify ways to cultivate intergenerational teamwork in your organization?

Are excited about the possibility of bringing Millennials onto your team?

Do you sometimes believe that Millennials are just latte-sipping, smartphone-toting hipsters?

If you answered yes to any of these questions, then this book is for you...

50 Things to Know About Working with Millennials by Isla Bishop offers an approach to understanding and improving complex intergenerational workplace dynamics. This book devolves into research which shapes the interpretation of Millennial behaviors while offering practical methods to attract, encourage, lead and communicate with younger employees.

So grab YOUR copy today. You'll be glad you did.

For each 50 Things to Know book that is sold (not including free days), 10 cents will be given to teaching and learning.

Isla Bishop

# TABLE OF CONTENTS

BOOK DESCRIPTION

TABLE OF CONTENTS

INTRODUCTION

1. Define "Generation"

2. Ignore the Stereotypes

3. Utilize the Technologically-Savvy

4. Harness their Creativity

5. Radiate Passion

6. Anticipate the Commitment Issues

7. Accept the Facts

8. Remember your Story

9. Provide Flexibility

10. Gain Perspective

11. Educate Them

12. Know the Financial Concerns

13. Explore New Opportunities

14. Recognize Work Ethic

15. Invest in Growth

16. Develop Corporate Responsibility Strategies

17. Examine your Patterns

18. Empower Them

19. Discuss the Dress Code

20. Understand the Culture

21. Cultivate Intergenerational Teamwork

23. Appreciate the Values-Driven Mentality

24. Get Curious

25. Expand the Conversation

26. Welcome Media

27. Create Structure

28. Identify the Multitaskers

29. Provide Feedback

30. Challenge Perceptions about Authority

31. Value Inclusion

32. Focus on Your Culture

33. Build Leadership Tracks

34. Embrace the Tatt

35. Cheer the Optimism

36. Support Content Creation

37. Reassess Career as Identity

38. Update your Systems

39. Acknowledge Humanity

40. Confront Issues Immediately

41. Inspire Excellence

42. Develop the Entrepreneurial Spirit

43. Consider the Similarities

44. Envision the Potential

45. Foster Meaningful Relationships

46. Instill Patience

47. Be Kind

48. Set the Example

49. Speak to Individual Needs

50. Allow Mistakes

## ABOUT THE AUTHOR

Isla is a Colorado-raised Storyteller and Project Specialist for a non-profit company. With a degree in Family Business and Humanities, she is passionate about using words to tell powerful stories and affect meaningful change. She believes it is important to engage in intergeneration dialogue that leads to mutual understanding, growth and healthy working environments.

Isla Bishop

# INTRODUCTION

*"Each generation imagines itself to be more intelligent than the one that went before it, and wiser than the one that comes after it."*

George Orwell

Entitled, overstimulated, and lacking in work ethic are all stereotypical terms used to define Millennials. But what does the research really say about this generation and their work habits? While some of these accusations may reflect truth, a more accurate description of this generation may be entrepreneurial, ethically-minded and resourceful.

For the first time, four unique generations are represented in the modern-day workplace. It is important to have conversations regarding intergenerational dynamics, communication preferences, values and career aspirations among your team. Generation Y is the largest and most diverse generation to date and recruiting young talent is crucial to the longevity of your organization.

Encouraging growth, rethinking your patterns and building intergenerational community will help both retain current employees and attract Millennials. As you understand some trends and statistics about the Millennial Generation, you will be able to create training programs, adjust corporate culture and inspire innovation. Whether you are a seasoned professional or another Millennial trying to gain credibility in the workplace, it is essential that you learn to work well with Millennials.

50 Things to Know

Isla Bishop

## 1. Define "Generation"

While the concept of generations was mentioned in ancient Egyptian and Greek texts, the modern study was influenced by German sociologist Karl Mannheim in the 1950's.[1] A "generation" is more than a group of people who share similar years of birth, it is the collective experience shaped by historical and social contexts. Traditionalists were shaped by the World Wars while Millennials grew up during 911 and the birth of the internet. These formative experiences establish worldviews, values, and common characteristics. However, there is a wide range of acceptable birth years that make up the Millennial generation and there are conflicting opinions about what makes them unique. Also, most research has been conducted in Western contexts and little is known about Millennial values internationally.[1]

## *2. Ignore the Stereotypes*

In some ways, Baby Boomers (born around 1946- 1964) and Generation Xers (born around 1965-1981) seem to be polar opposites of Millennials (born around 1982-2000). Yet, it is impossible to generalize a group of 1.8 billion people across the globe[3] or over 80 million United States citizens[9]. Studies on generational differences are inconsistent and many scholars have questioned whether these stereotypes actually exist in the workplace.[1] Other factors like socioeconomic class, gender, religion, personality and life stage may play bigger roles in workplace dynamics than generational differences. There are a few key generational trends that can help paint a general picture of how a Millennial *may* behave in work situations, but it is critical to remember that all Millennials are not technological wizards just like all Baby Boomers are not workaholics.

### 3. Utilize the Technologically-Savvy

Communication and technology aptitude and application is one of the most undisputed generational differences.[1] As digital natives, the "Look at Me" generation most self-identifies with technology use.[16] About half say they sent or received a text message over the phone in the past day, approximately double the proportion of Generation Xers.[8] They are experienced with communication technologies, the internet, computer programs, phone applications and social media— and they know it. This technological know-how can be beneficial as you dream up new strategies to better achieve your mission.

### 4. Harness their Creativity

You don't need to have arcades or sleeping pods to get creative (although, working at Google wouldn't be awful).[13] From idea-generating field trips to Pixar's "personal project days" where employees are given time to work on whatever they want to, there are lots of ways to encourage originality in the workplace.[2] Studies suggest, based on their age and unique experiences, Millennials tend to demonstrate more outside-of-the-box thinking and are more prone to challenge norms which could lead to some great breakthroughs for your office.[1]

## 5. Radiate Passion

If you are a leader, it's your responsibility and privilege to invite your team into your vision. Bill Hybels, author of *Courageous Leadership* and founder of the Global Leadership Summit, says "It's your job to keep your passion hot. Do whatever you have to do, read whatever you have to read, go wherever you have to go to stay fired up."[6] That kind of passion is contagious. As a leader, you get to set the tone of your company. As Michael Jordan said, "Earn your leadership every day".

## 6. Anticipate the Commitment Issues

Disloyalty is one of the biggest complaints about Generation Y. Baby Boomers value hard work and consistency while Millennials (and Generation Xers) thrive in environments of change, career mobility and flexibility. They are more motivated by a cause than a specific business and 91% tend to stay with a company for less than 3 years.[9] In fact, the average Millennial will hold 7 different jobs by age 26.[11]

However, it is important not to discount life stage while discussing company loyalty. In general, loyalty towards employers has decreased over each generation.[15] This is more likely to reflect the fact that humans tend to prefer the familiar and seek stability with increased age and responsibility. The idea of learning a new trade and socializing with a new group of people is often less appealing at a later life stage.[15] Some studies argue that Millennials' loyalty is comparable to other generations at similar ages.[15] Regardless of the reasons, it is important to note that Millennials tend to switch frequently between companies. But there are ways to combat this higher turnover intention. On top of offering fair compensation and challenging work, companies that invest in career development, mentorship opportunities and increased employee engagement are better able to retain Millennials.[1]

## 7. Accept the Facts

Before designing training programs or filling roles on your team, it may be helpful to identify some of facts about Millennials. 34% of Millennials have at least a bachelor's degree which makes them the most educated generation to date.[14] This level of education can make them seem overly-confident or even entitled. However, their unemployment rate is almost double that of the US average which may lead to a greater desire for stable positions.[11] Most studies agree that they value team work, diversity, flexibility, training, and work-life balance.[15]

## 8. Remember your Story

Reminiscing about your own past and experiences may help you empathize with Millennials. When you were 25, what were you struggling with or learning? Who were some role models in your life and how did they motivate and inspire you? Also be sensitive to the fact that these young people *aren't you*. They have unique backgrounds, fears and passions, so don't project your own experiences onto them. You may have walked up a hill, in the snow, *both ways* when you were a kid, but recognize that every generation has its own struggles on top of the normal age-related challenges.

## 9. Provide Flexibility

Millennials value flexibility in work hours, communication and types of tasks. Working remotely is becoming more common across every generation and a majority of Millennials want to be able to set their own work hours.[9] They also balance work and life more fluidly than Baby Boomers who prefer a clear division between personal and professional.[1] The use of technological tools

Isla Bishop

has impacted communication and evolved the ability to multitask life and work projects simultaneously. Some studies suggest that the trend towards more accommodating work schedules is intergenerational.[1] Allowing flexibility is attractive to prospective employees of all ages and may lead to higher job satisfaction. As long as the job is getting done well, a more relaxed work schedule could be worth considering.

50 Things to Know

*"Millennials aspire to marry the blue skies thinking of the Boomers with the grass-roots mindset of GenX."*

*Mal Fletcher*

## 10. Gain Perspective

Every person operates from a different worldview and these disparities seem more significant when multiplied across generational lines. Millennials have been criticized for not sharing the same opinions about time, company allegiance or work ethic as their older colleagues. However, they simply view and define workplace success differently. Learning to motivate and relate to the Millennials in your workplace may help provide long-term sustainability.

## 11. Educate Them

For a variety of reasons, "real life" looks different to Millennials than to older generations when they were similar ages. 1 out of 10 Millennials will buy a home before age 30.[11] 1 in 5 are married and only 12% have children.[11] They are getting married and starting families later than their predecessors.[7] This may be a reflection on soaring divorce rates or the rising average amount of student debt which make marriage and parenthood seem unappealing or impossible. There is also a greater focus, especially for women, on developing careers younger. Regardless, Millennials could use guidance from their elders in navigating the real world as they mature as employees, spouses, parents and adults in general.

## 12. Know the Financial Concerns

In 2011, more than 50% of Millennials had over $35,000 in student loan debt.[16] Most of Generation Y believes that they will never see a pension or receive money from Social Security.[1] In light of this enormous fiscal burden, younger employees are craving both job security and financial wisdom. You could attract Millennials by offering 401k packages, providing financial seminars and creating partnerships with universities to lower degree costs. Also be sure that the required degree listed in the job description reflects the position's pay scale, an internship or assistant position should not necessitate a master's degree.

## 13. Explore New Opportunities

Millennials work well on teams—take advantage of their

willingness to jump in! Have you been thinking about creating a summer spirit week to boost company morale or starting a volleyball team to build community? Look to the Millennials to provide ideas and enthusiasm for these projects.

## *14. Recognize Work Ethic*

Some studies have found that Generation Y has a higher work ethic than their older counterparts, some say Millennials are lazy and most agree that there is relatively no difference in work ethic between generations.[1] The stereotype is that younger generations do not work as hard nor care as much about their work.[15] However, the reality is that work ethic is affected by education level, life stage, work status (full or part-time), employee engagement, income level and marital status.[15] Regardless of generation bracket, those with low incomes or those who were married tended to report stronger work ethic.[15] Perceived work ethic also depends on how work is defined. Baby Boomers are more process-oriented and value long hours while younger generations tend to adopt the "work smarter" mentality.[15] They are more focused on achieving great results and less interested in the process. Millennials may also be more satisfied as well as productive if they are able to work flexibly according to their schedule. If you emphasize your standards and expectations and make sure all deadlines are respected, Millennials should perform well.

## 15. Invest in Growth

If you can create a loyal employee and shape them as a future leader in your company, you win. If Millennials are given opportunities to grow and gain valuable skills, they win. One of the highest priorities for Millennials is coaching, yet according to Forbes, only 7% of organizations invested in coaching, mentoring or dedicated time with senior leadership.[4] Younger generations are placing higher importance on learning opportunities than older generations and they are interested in companies that are willing to invest in their growth. Consider scheduling weekly "Grow Time", bringing in professionals from other fields for workshops, connecting new employees with veterans or even investing in training resources like online learning programs or conferences.

## 16. Develop Corporate Responsibility Strategies

57% of Millennials volunteer regularly and 75% donate to nonprofits.[11] They are not as selfish as presumed and are looking to work for organizations that are making a meaningful impact on their communities. Companies that develop a corporate social responsibility mission, match donations, focus on their values and encourage employees to serve will be very desirable.

## 17. Examine your Patterns

Innovative companies are not content with doing things the same way because "that's the way we've always done it." Twenty- and thirtysomethings may bring fresh insight to old routines. Welcome change and empower your team to think creatively.

## 18. Empower Them

Ed Catmull, Pixar Animation Studios and Walt Disney Animation Studios, says the wrong question is "how do we prevent our people from screwing up?" The better question which leads to greater creativity is "how do we enable our people to solve problems?"[2] Your youngest employees bring innovation, ingenuity and perspective and when these Millennials are empowered, they can transform your company. One way Millennials feel empowered is when their opinions are heard and their work recognized. Unlike Baby Boomers, they value routine and informal recognition.[1]

## 19. Discuss the Dress Code

79% of Millennials believe jeans are acceptable work attire versus 60% of Boomers.[16] Older generations tend to assign higher value to standard views of professionalism and Baby Boomers believe respecting rules and codes of conduct is very important. However, Millennials find fun and stimulation at work to be more significant. One study found that the more compliant Baby Boomers had fewer terminations than Millennials which may be connected to views on obeying rules.[1] Not all Millennials sport baggy t-shirts and canvas shoes to work. But if they do, it may be a good time to clarify your dress code.

## 20. Understand the Culture

Millennials are very connected. One average, a they will check their phone 43 times per day and this "always on" mentality can be useful.[18] Task them with maintaining brand awareness, communicating with customers and building relationships with potential clients.

## 21. Cultivate Intergenerational Teamwork

Open communication is critical in a working environment. Adopting mutual support, understanding and dialogue among generations will build greater trust, deeper relationships and higher job satisfaction.[1] Baby Boomers are especially concerned with building cohesion and positive social interactions in the work place.[1] Similarly, Millennials thrive in team environments and tend to enjoy collaborative work.

**50 Things to Know**

Isla Bishop

*"Don't lie to anyone, but particularly don't lie to Millennials. They just know. They can smell it. Be yourself: if you're old, be old. If you don't know anything about pop culture, don't pretend to know anything about pop culture. When you credit [Millennials] with intelligence and emotional sophistication, they respond intelligently and with emotional sophistication."*

*John Green*

## 22. Mentor Them

A study by Bellevue University found that both mentors and mentees have over a 20% higher retention rate, saving about $6.7 million in human resources costs.[1] Creating mentorship opportunities can benefit everyone involved while building greater community and improved communication. Statistics confirm that all generations tend to view strong relationships between supervisors and employees as an important indicator of overall work well-being and training satisfaction.[1] But Millennials are specifically relying on this relationship to provide guidance.[1]

## 23. Appreciate the Values-Driven Mentality

12% of Baby Boomers said meaningful work was important to them versus 30% of Millennials.[1] Millennials tend to pursue personal development, fulfillment and the ability to make a meaningful contribution. Some studies have found that the desire for authenticity is especially important as Millennials want to work for a company that aligns with their personal values.[1] Organizations that are value-based will be more attractive.

## 24. Get Curious

Ask good questions. Every Millennial has a unique personality, communication style, skill set and motivation. Before assuming what they want or need, ask them how they feel about their job, what tasks they don't enjoy and if they believe their skills are being well utilized. Also have them reflect on their career aspirations, what they bring to the team and which work routines are most productive. Identifying and developing these strengths and habits will serve everyone involved.

## 25. Expand the Conversation

Most Millennials are hyper-engaged and highly value teamwork. Adopting a more open culture of communication and allowing all levels of employee input will help a Millennial find meaning in their work. Often, businesses are made up of silos and departments. But successful companies are recognizing the importance of developing interdepartmental (and intergenerational) conversations as this lead to greater community and innovation.[2] Encouraging conversations may also prevent conflict and misunderstanding.

## 26. Welcome Media

Younger generations are more familiar with all forms of media. They may be aware of applications and programs which could spice up your meetings or transform your presentations. Be open to trying new things! While Millennials are widely regarded as more proficient with technology, research indicates that Boomers and Xers equally value (and are not resistant to) the use of technology in the workplace and are not resistant to technology.[1]

## 27. Create Structure

In 2017, the youngest Millennials are just entering adulthood. On top of all the normal "adult things" like transitioning away from microwave meals and applying for auto loans, they may be learning what is appropriate behavior in the office. You can help by clearly defining expectations. Studies show that Millennials want to be part of the decision-making process, desire clear expectations for success and value organized work settings. This isn't ground-breaking science and is pretty standard among generations. However, if these preferences are absent from the workplace, it may result in higher levels of dissatisfaction and turnover.[1]

## 28. Identify the Multitaskers

Multitasking is the way of the 21st century and this style of work can create both opportunity and harm. This style of work is natural and prevalent for Millennials who may often be juggling multiple projects simultaneously over several different devices.[1] Remind them to slow down and focus on quality.

## 29. Provide Feedback

Author and former presidential speechwriter, James Humes, said, "The art of communication is the language of leadership." Millennials desire to engage deeply and a majority want constant feedback, so having an approachable relationship with coworkers and supervisors is critical. 80% want constant feedback from their managers.[16] This expectation of immediate evaluation may be uncomfortable for older generations who see uninhibited communication as earned based on age and experience.[12]

## 30. Challenge Perceptions about Authority

Unlike Baby Boomers who viewed managers as experts, Millennials have grown up with accessible information at their fingertips.[1] They view managers as coaches and are used to open communication, collaborative working environments and egalitarian structures. Both Xers and Millennials are not impressed or intimated by titles and feel that respect from superiors needs to be earned.[15] They have been taught to ask questions and be critical of information. This comfort with authority can be interpreted as entitlement or disrespect; however, other scholars argue that generations do not have widely different views of "formal authority".[1] Depending on your corporate culture, you may need to address these perceptions of authority.

Isla Bishop

50 Things to Know

Isla Bishop

*"When we say Millennials, what we mean is people that are younger than us."* Scott Stratten

**50 Things to Know**

## 31. Value Inclusion

Self-identified as tolerant and democratic, Millennials desire equality in the workplace.[9] They may struggle with traditional leadership structures and advocate for intergenerational inclusion regardless of rank. Millennials are the most diverse generation to date and, thanks to technology, they are the first "global generation".[1] Some scholars rate diversity as one of the top motivational factors in the Millennial's job hunt.[1]

## 32. Focus on Your Culture

Corporate culture is becoming a more prevalent discussion among high-performing businesses. As the concept of work is evolving, employees desire enjoyable work spaces. Millennials value workplace "play" more than previous generations and positively associate fun with happiness and high performance.[1] How can your organization infuse fun into everyday work?

## 33. Build Leadership Tracks

In 2025, nearly 75% of the U.S. workforce will be made up by

Millennials.[18] Some companies, such as Enterprise Rent-A-Car are investing in Millennials as the leaders of the future. The world's largest car rental company promotes internally, hires 60-70% Millennials and provides ample leadership training opportunities.[4] With a stronger desire for quicker promotion, younger generations are thirsty for leadership experience that will help them boost their careers.[1] Companies that provide a clear advancement track will have an advantage over those that do not offer growth opportunities.

## 34. Embrace the Tatt

Between a third to a half of Millennials have a tattoo, dyed their hair a non-traditional color or have pierced something other than their ear lobe.[8] For this generation, body art is less taboo than in other generations. Freedom of expression has become more prevalent in Western cultures and a tattoo no longer equates to unprofessional. If tattoos are banned in your rulebook, you may want to rethink the reasoning, unless of course the tattoo is offensive.

## 35. Cheer the Optimism

Over 88% of Millennials said they were optimistic about the future of their career versus 76% of Generation Xers.[16] This hopeful perspective is inspiring, but optimism can be both a strength and a weakness. Older employees have less idealized views of work so this perspective may seem unrealistic.[15] But it can also infuse fresh confidence into your team. Help the Millennials invest in their futures so they can achieve their career aspirations and propel your organization forward.

## 36. Support Content Creation

As both heavy media consumers and content producers, Millennials could help publish content that drives traffic to your website or blog. On average, they switch between media platforms 27 times a day and over 75% have a social networking profile.[11] They understand the world of WordPress and Twitter and have a sense of good marketing techniques. These employees can be assets as you develop your brand on social media platforms. Add 'content creation' to the job description and let them do their thing.

## 37. Reassess Career as Identity

A "career" is an important characterization for Baby Boomers who are known for working 50- 60 hour weeks. But for Millennials in general, work is less central to their identities and they have a greater sense of work-life balance.[12] Over the generations, the central importance of work is declining while the desire for more leisure time to pursue personal hobbies or relationships is increasing.[1] Xers and Millennials do not believe job performance is tied to an individual's worth.[15] If a Millennial won the lottery, they would more likely quit their job while a Boomer would feel obligated to continue to work.[1]

## 38. Update your Systems

Outdated platforms, CRMs and servers may have worked for you for decades, but improving technology could save time and money as well as keep Millennials engaged. To young employees, a work environment with the latest technology is critical.[1] Ask them if they know of any online solutions or applications which could help improve work flow. Leave it to a Millennial to find a faster, easier way to accomplish a task.

## 39. Acknowledge Humanity

Millennials are parents, pilots, college students, nomads, veterans, artists, unemployed, congressmen and billionaires. They are humans— women and men, introverts and extroverts, rich and poor— with hopes, fears and goals. Like their parents and grandparents, they are balancing work, life, and relationships. Always remember that regardless of age, everyone is valuable and worthy of respect.

**50 Things to Know**

Isla Bishop

*"I can do things you cannot, you can do things I cannot; together we can do great things"*

*Mother Teresa*

50 Things to Know

## 40. Confront Issues Immediately

If there is dissention, miscommunication or negative vibes in the workplace, address the problem directly. Regardless of age, some employees are difficult to work with and thrive off of drama. Some may even have negative intentions. If a Millennial is truly entitled, defiant or disloyal, take immediate action before the situation gets exponentially worse. A negative team member can quickly lead to destroyed morale, the loss of valuable staff and decreased productivity. Confrontation should be kind, private, direct and clear.

## 41. Inspire Excellence

Millennials have grown up with Kid President and TED talks. They are familiar with captivating content and desire influential leaders to infuse passion into their daily work. These young creatives are ready to be inspired!

You could add 5 minutes to your team meetings dedicated to sharing inspiration that will drive healthy perspectives, refocus on your mission and encourage excellence.

## 42. Develop the Entrepreneurial Spirit

59% of Millennials want to or already are starting their own business.[16] They value meaningful tasks with intrinsic rewards and are willing to work in unconventional ways. This could be a great opportunity to invite creative ideas, generate innovative projects and allow Millennials the chance to develop leadership skills while engaging their entrepreneurial inclinations.

## 43. Consider the Similarities

While there are many generational differences, there are also a lot of similarities that help form a mutual foundation of understanding. Studies indicate that all generations value job stability, competitive compensation, challenging work and good working conditions.[1] Employees want to make a different at their company. Like other generations, most Millennials value strong work ethic, have career goals and are juggling everyday life challenges. Finding and emphasizing common ground could help bridge relational gaps.

## *44. Envision the Potential*

Generation Y is more familiar with group projects and open office spaces rather than the traditional beige-walled "cubical land". Be open to trying new things in regards to your space. Young companies like Emma are opting for the less-traditional office layout and are moving towards more collaborative, creative spaces.

## *45. Foster Meaningful Relationships*

Transitioning from a world of constant exposure to technology and social media to the navigation of daily work interactions may induce some culture shock. However, Millennials desire authentic relationships and they are just as likely as older coworkers to value traditional in-person communication.[1] In general, physical face-to-face forms of communication are declining with increased technological options across every generation.[1] So it is even more important to focus on building work relationships and encouraging employee engagement to help acquire and retain valuable employees.[5]

## 46. Instill Patience

In a world of Google, Siri and Amazon Prime, practicing patience is an art. Millennials have been trained to expect instant gratification while older generations value rank and have earned their promotions. Like every previous generation, the new kids on the block need to be taught patience and work ethic. Research suggests that mastering a job can take up to 10,000 hours or 5 years so patience is really is key.[16]

## 47. Be Kind

The timeless apothegm prevails— "do unto others as you would have them do unto you." This rule is golden for a reason. According to Plato, we should be kind, "for everyone you meet is fighting a hard battle."

## 48. Set the Example

Do you feel like your coworkers or employees are acting entitled? Are they inseparable from their phones? Show them a different way. Sending memos or posting rules next to the refrigerator will not be as effective as personally modeling appropriate behaviors.

## 49. Speak to Individual Needs

Some people need their strengths to be affirmed before they can hear criticism while others abhor "fluff" and don't need to be nurtured. This has more to do with culture and personality than age. Investing in personality tests for the department and spending time discussing how personalities may affect team dynamics could be extremely beneficial. Some great tests are StrengthsFinder, Myers Briggs Type Indicator, Enneagram, VIA Character Strengths, the "5 Minute Lion-Otter-Golden Retriever-Beaver Test", DiSC Assessment and Leading from your Strengths. Most of these tests identify an individual's strengths weaknesses, relationship approach, preferred way to give and receive information, motivators, workplace habits and natural versus adapted habits. Plus, it's fun to know who is more of a beaver and who is the office otter.

## 50. Allow Mistakes

Design an inspiring environment which encourages curiosity. Younger employees need experience, mentorship and the opportunity to contribute. If an environment is too critical and uncomfortable, Millennials may seek work elsewhere.

Isla Bishop

https://www.nimh.nih.gov/health/statistics/prevalence/any-anxiety-disorder-among-adults.shtml

https://www.adaa.org/sites/default/files/GAD_depression_symptoms%20overlap.pdf

https://www.adaa.org/living-with-anxiety/women/facts

https://www.adaa.org/living-with-anxiety/children/anxiety-and-depression

https://www.nimh.nih.gov/health/publications/teen-depression/index.shtml

http://www.mayoclinic.org/diseases-conditions/mental-illness/basics/risk-factors/con-20033813

http://www.mayoclinic.org/diseases-conditions/mental-illness/basics/treatment/con-20033813

http://www.rcpsych.ac.uk/mentalhealthinformation/therapies/cognitivebehaviouraltherapy.aspx

http://www.health.harvard.edu/mind-and-mood/relaxation-techniques-breath-control-helps-quell-errant-stress-response

http://www.psychology-solution.com/sleep-insomnia/anxiety-depression

Isla Bishop

http://www.mayoclinic.org/diseases-conditions/depression/in-depth/depression-and-exercise/art-20046495

http://eo2.commpartners.com/users/counseling/downloads/130724_Slides.pdf

http://www.mayoclinic.org/diseases-conditions/depression/basics/complications/con-20032977

http://www.everydayhealth.com/hs/major-depression/depression-memory-loss-and-concentration/

http://www.mind.org.uk/information-support/types-of-mental-health-problems/depression/self-care-for-depression/#challenge

http://www.webmd.com/depression/guide/diet-recovery#2

http://www.mayoclinic.org/diseases-conditions/panic-attacks/basics/causes/con-20020825

http://articles.mercola.com/sites/articles/archive/2013/12/05/anxiety.aspx

http://www.health.harvard.edu/staying-healthy/anxiety_and_physical_illness

http://psychcentral.com/blog/archives/2013/01/28/using-mindfulness-to-treat-anxiety-disorders/

http://www.webmd.com/balance/stress-management/stress-management-doing-progressive-muscle-relaxation

http://www.mayoclinic.org/tests-procedures/meditation/in-depth/meditation/art-20045858

www.ingramcontent.com/pod-product-compliance
Lightning Source LLC
Chambersburg PA
CBHW020710180526
45163CB00008B/3016